DIGITAL MARKETING BEATS

Know the latest statistics & trends for business & career growth in 2020. Make a difference.

TARANNUM KHAN

DIGITAL MARKETING BEATS

By Tarannum Khan

Website: www.digitaltarannum.com
Contact Info: info@digitaltarannum.com
Academy: https://www.digitaltarannum.com/digital-tarannum-academy/
Courses: https://www.digitaltarannum.com/courses/

Preface

Digital Marketing Beats provides a base for learning digital marketing based on current statistics, marketing trends, and reports. This marketing book is designed to enable holistic learning for entrepreneurs and professionals. The main aim is to enhance the chances of the success rate of start-ups and careers. Five sections of this book include:

- **Section 1:** Growth of business and career with digital marketing and upcoming opportunities in digital marketing channels

- **Section 2:** Latest marketing statistics (2017-2019) and its effects on strategies

- **Section 3:** Marketing trends 2019-2020 and how to use them in a marketing plan

- **Section 4:** Growing career opportunities in 2019-2020 and certifications

- **Section 5:** Top branding and money-making methods for 2019-2020

About the Author

Tarannum Khan is a passionate and proactive marketer, blogger, author, educationist, and speaker having more than 8 years of experience in the field of marketing.

Digital Marketing Beats is a dedicated book for digital marketing enthusiasts who want to be updated with knowledge and have a core interest in learning. The book is for digital marketing aspirants and entrepreneurs who wish to push their career and business to the next level of success.

Regards,
Tarannum
www.digitaltarannum.com

Table of Contents

Introduction

As an entrepreneur, it becomes essential to understand digital marketing to make the best choices for your business.

If you have followed traditional marketing for a very long time, then it is of utmost importance to understand how to reach your audience globally. Digital marketing is for all. Learn to explore and have reasons to follow.

When you go by other's suggestions, it may be right for you, but having your reasoning improves the chances of your success.

You should have reasons to choose each channel to start your work. From the past decades, there is a shift from traditional marketing to digital marketing.

If you are interested in starting your career in digital marketing, then it is a must to understand the core of the digital marketing field. It will help to evaluate your potential and will let you choose the best option.

Digital Marketing, as a part of marketing, pinpoints the use of digital marketing for any business or brand.

Generally, two terms are often used– **Internet Marketing/Online Marketing** and **Digital Marketing** but are they synonymous? If not, how?

In simple words, digital marketing uses both online and offline channels, but Internet Marketing includes online channels only.

It is a booming industry and there are a large number of online audiences beyond boundaries. You need to choose the right platform to connect.

In this digital life, every marketer goes through the same phase during the initial period. A systematic approach to learning digital marketing will be the best way for beginners, professionals, or entrepreneurs. So never hesitate to explore.

Digital marketing channels include:

- Search Engine Optimization (SEO)
- Pay Per Click | Google Ads | Online Display Advertising (SEM)
- Social Media Marketing (SMM)
- Email Marketing
- E-commerce Marketing
- Content Marketing and Inbound Marketing
- App Marketing
- Affiliate Marketing
- Radio Marketing

- TV Marketing
- Mobile Marketing
- Electronic Billboards

Marketing

Statistics &

Metrics

Marketing Statistics (2017–2019)

Here the reasons that will support your choice.

According to HubSpot, the latest insights of marketing statistics are:

- **Embedded videos** on landing pages are going to increase conversions by **86%**. (Wordstream, 2018)

- **Google** itself drives **96%** of the mobile search traffic. (Jody Nimetz Co., 2018)

- **Organic search results** are the priority of **70-80%** of search engine users. (MarTech, 2018)

- Videos are the first choice. It is likely to drive **50 times more** organic traffic in comparison to plain text. (Omnicore, 2018)

- By 2020, **50%** of all online searches will be **voice searches**. (Wordstream, 2018)

- **The top inbound marketing** priority of **55%** of marketers is blog content creation. (HubSpot, 2018)

- **India** has the **largest base of Facebook users** in comparison to any other country in the world. (Statitsa, 2018)

According to Statista Marketing Statistics,

- **Ad spending** in the digital advertising market amounts to **US$98,247m** in 2019. (Worldwide)

- With a market volume of **US$112,297m** in 2019, most ad spending is generated in the United States.

- **Global Comparison** of the top five countries with the most ad spending in digital advertising shows that the United States - US $ 112,297m, China - US $ 57,898m, United Kingdom - US $ 20,737m, Japan - US $ 12,790m, and Germany - US $ 8,706m. (2019)

- Revenue in the digital media market amounts to **US$2,285m** in 2019. (India)

- **Revenue in the digital media** market amounts to **US$151,966m** in 2019. (Worldwide)

- The market's largest segment is **video games**, with a market volume of **US$83,169m** in 2019. (Worldwide)

- As of July 2019, **1.6 billion users** were accessing the WhatsApp messenger every month.

As per HubSpot Marketing Statistics,

- **61% of mobile searchers** are more likely to contact a local business if they have a mobile-friendly site. (Junto, 2019)

- **86%** of people look up the location of a business on Google Maps. (Junto, 2019)

- **50%** of search queries are four words or longer. (IMPACT, 2019)

- Voice is expected to be a **$40 billion** channel by 2022. (OC&C Strategy Consultants, 2019)

- **65%** of 25-49-year old's speak to their voice-enabled devices at least once a day. (PWC, 2019)

- Marketers who prioritize **blogging efforts** are 13x more likely to see positive ROI. (HubSpot, 2019)

- **51% of B2B marketers** prioritize creating visual assets as part of their content marketing strategy. (HubSpot, 2019)

- **Listicles** are the most popular blog post format among business blogs. (Responsive Inbound Marketing, 2019)

- Globally, there are over **2.38 billion** monthly active users on Facebook. (Facebook, 2019)

- LinkedIn has over **500 million** users. (LinkedIn, 2019)

- Facebook is the **second most-used platform** globally, followed by YouTube. (Pew Research Center, 2019)

- **71%** of Instagram users are under the age of 35. (Statitsa, 2019)

- More than **500 million** people use Instagram every day. (Oberlo, 2019)

- Instagram has over **1 billion** active monthly users. (Oberlo, 2019)

- There are **2.77 billion** social media users globally. (Statitsa, 2019)

- **Active email accounts** are expected to hit **5.6 billion** this year. (Statitsa, 2019)

- **Mobile readers** who open an email a second time from a computer are 65% more likely to click through. (Campaign Monitor, 2019)

- **91%** of shoppers want to hear from companies they do business with via email. (Sleeknote, 2019)

- **49%** of people said they click on text ads. (Blue Corona, 2019)

- **63%** of people said they'd click on a Google ad. (Search Engine Land, 2019)

- A delay of one second in **mobile page response** can reduce conversions by 7%. (99 Firms, 2019)

Impact of Digital Marketing Trends

Latest Digital Marketing Trends

The penetration of the internet and social media in our lives is steadily increasing. It is an excellent avenue for small businesses to take advantage of rising digital marketing trends.

After having reviewed the trends in digital marketing from the past few years, I have enlisted the top digital marketing trends that you need to follow for better business performance.

Digital marketing is the trendiest phase of the marketing world, yet, even this phase has some methods and patterns that we should track every year.

The top trends in digital marketing are:

Social Media

We all are active on social media. Also, you might have come across those business stories that people share on social media platforms.

These stories include social matters, proud stories, and success stories of personalities and businesses.

It is the perfect platform for customer engagement and brand promotion.

Instagram Marketing – Instagram Stories, Instagram Live, and IGTV

Instagram has hit around more than 2 billion users in recent years. You should try IGTV as one of your marketing strategies.

Create video content on your Instagram account. Make sure that it is too compelling and impactful.

Facebook Messenger Marketing – Use ChatBots

It is one of the trending marketing tools so far. Use ChatBots to increase customer reach like MobileMonkey.

It enhances the customer experience and better customer engagement. Your customers can use these real-time ChatBots to resolve the queries.

LinkedIn Marketing – Economical Costing

Reduced ad costing has enhanced opportunities for B2B businesses to use LinkedIn in 2019 and 2020. It is the right time to use LinkedIn ads.

Influencer Marketing

Influencer marketing is another impactful digital marketing trend.

Have you ever heard of brand ambassadors? Yes,

influencer marketing is somewhat similar to it. Use top personalities and celebrities to promote your brand and see its positive impacts.

"As one of the top digital marketing trends, Instagram influencer marketing can raise your sales graph.

YouTube influencer marketing can be a game-changer, so try this too. Videos are very impactful, so go ahead with YouTube."

Voice Search

Make your website voice search ready. The Google Assistant and Apple's Siri are the best examples of such digital marketing trends.

Create a script that would match all customer queries and requirements. Yes, for sure, it is going to impress your customers.

Video Content

Videos have always created a significant impact. Create useful video content for web pages or social media accounts.

When the audience likes those videos, they will inevitably start following your business as well.

You can use apps and software to make engaging videos. Brands are recording live videos to connect with their audience.

It should be clear that you are creating content for your viewers to make it more engaging.

Email Marketing

Old is Gold! Email marketing is the oldest trend but is still working for the majority of the businesses.

Make use of this digital marketing trend and see the impact on your business. Startups, bloggers, and small businesses can use email marketing as the best tool to drive more sales.

"Here's a fun fact for you, according to Statista, the number of email users is set to grow to about 4.3 billion users in 2022. (A marked increase from 3.7 billion in 2017)".

So, what does this mean? Well, the potential in email marketing is pretty high and it's up to you to take advantage of it. An excellent way to do this is by using email marketing services.

Augmented Reality

If you want to get the best ROIs for all the marketing

strategies, then this is the right trend that you should consider.

Remember, the game Pokémon Go? It is the best example of augmented reality.

Artificial Intelligence

When programmatic advertising to target specific users integrates with artificial intelligence makes the ad placements better.

AI is a lucrative career for professionals. Once you know the digital marketing trends, you can take your business to new heights or grow your career in different areas of digital marketing.

Career Opportunities & Certifications (2019-20)

Latest Jobs in Digital Marketing

Digital marketing is now the current trend in marketing today. This transition to digital marketing is caused by the fact that consumers have changed how they make purchases.

No wonder it is expected that companies would increase their digital marketing spending by up to 12.3 percent in about a year. It makes a career in digital marketing quite attractive.

Digital marketing offers numerous lucrative career choices, especially in countries like the United States & India. Many career opportunities in digital marketing that exist today were not available a few years ago. Let's see some of these careers.

SEO Specialists

SEO (Search Engine Optimization) is an integral part of digital marketing, making it a hot spot for a career in digital marketing. SEO helps businesses to increase their customer base by improving their visibility.

Email Marketing Specialist

Email marketing is another marketing strategy that is still on the rise. An email-marketing expert is in high demand because they are well versed in content creation, content delivery, editing, and copywriting.

UX Designer

User experience (UX) defines how your site or blog relates to your customers. UX designers design marketing apps and websites.

UX designers are in high demand because of their technical know-how in designing.

Content Managers

Content is the soul of any blog, so it is quite understandable that content managers would be in high demand, especially in a country like India. Content managers understand how to create insightful and engaging content that is SEO-friendly.

"Social Media Marketing Expert, Affiliate Marketers, Google Ads Experts, Brand Manager, Business Analytics Specialist, Web Designer, Professional Blogger, Mobile Marketing Specialist, Email Marketer, and Search Experts are the most searched jobs."

Digital Marketing has a lot of opportunities for everyone, including creative thinkers, business people, and technology gurus. Digital marketing is an excellent career choice because there is a high demand for people with digital marketing proficiency.

If you are looking to pursue a career in digital

marketing, then you need to figure out the best aspect of digital marketing for yourself. Gain knowledge of this area and develop yourself gradually.

Digital marketing also offers numerous mini choices that you can focus on and start working on it.

It is more advisable to focus on these areas than taking digital marketing as a whole. Digital marketing allows you to be creative while earning your money.

The most popular areas of digital marketing are SEO, content managing, email marketing, and so on.

Getting a job in digital marketing may be quite tricky; there are job sites that can help you get the best opportunities quickly.

> *"If you are looking for digital marketing jobs, then visit sites like Indeed.com, Monster.com, CareerBuilder.com, Shine.com, Naukri.com, SimplyHired.com, TimesJob.com, LinkedIn, Glassdoor.com, and so on."*

Digital marketers are one of the most sought-after professionals because of the proliferation of blogs and sites.

Choosing a career in digital marketing involves a proper determination of which aspect you should focus on and taking necessary steps to improve your knowledge and skills.

Certifications for Professionals

The certifications for beginners and advanced learners are:

Google Ads Search Certification	Google Ads Display Certification
Google Ads-Measurement Certification	Google Ads Video Certification
Display and Video 360 Certification	Search Ads 360 Certification
Campaign Manager Certification	Creative Certification
Google Analytics Individual Qualification	HubSpot Academy
Google My Business Basics	Waze Ads Certifications
Shopping Ads Certification	Bing Ads Certification
Facebook Blueprint Certification	Kameleoon A/B Testing
Twitter Flight School Certification	Lynda

Now, know more in-depth about the **Digital Marketing Channels** and decide your success path.

Search Engine

Optimization

Organic Search Results

Why is search engine optimization so important? Yes, It is. The organic search result is significant for any website. When you start your journey to learn SEO, the knowledge in bits and pieces makes you more confused and is often time-consuming.

Why & How puts a lot of pressure and you begin to read a lot about search engine optimization but the best suggestion is to be a data-driven marketer.

Data analysis and a list of synchronized actions can lead to better SEO results with average efforts rather than investing a lot of time on one technique.

It's a lengthy procedure and your result cannot be determined in a week. But dedicated efforts will give the desired results.

Why start learning SEO blindly? Make a synchronized pattern to understand SEO. It is essential to know SEO deeply to understand how important it is to get a higher ranking in Google search results and other search engines.

"Search Engine Optimization can be very well explained as the process of optimizing the visibility of a website/web page in a search engine's unpaid results for a certain keyword."

When anyone performs a search query, Search Engine Optimization contributes to a higher web page rank in the SERP.

Importance of SEO

SEO is important as the ultimate goal is to appear on the first page of Google; this drives traffic and converts into the leads.

- **SEO Strategies**: Better SEO strategies makes the website user-friendly

- **Credibility:** Users' blog sharing, likes, and comments improve the reliability of a website

- **Outperformance:** Better optimized websites bury competitor's SEO strategy and improve sales

As per Google Algorithm, these high priority criteria you should include to optimizing your website:

Mobile-First Indexing: Google dominates on mobile search results and it has more than 90% of market share. Now, it's time for mobile-friendly websites, so you need to take care of your website parameters.

Voice Search: Voice search is a game-changer. Nowadays, voice search is a more natural way to search on Google and YouTube.

Content and Links: Content is king. Well written content and high-quality link building improve your ranking chances.

Video Marketing: YouTube videos, Facebook videos, and other kinds of promotional videos will add advantage to website ranking. It improves website ranking and credibility among users. Podcasts will help you in building links.

User Experience Signal: Visitor's experience to a website also signals to the ranking factor. Now, improve your user experience to get a better Google ranking.

On-page & Off-page Techniques

- **Tags & Titles:** In-depth keyword analysis for writing a title and use of keywords in H1, H2, H3 tags appropriately.

- **Great Content:** Just good content won't be enough; you need great content to drive traffic. The content should be in context. Improve your site's dwell time and update outdated content.

- **Meta Description:** Meta descriptions should be well defined for each page and should be a summary.

- **Images:** Optimize, compress & rename the images as per keywords and fill ALT Tags for images.

- **Mobile Friendliness:** Web pages should be responsive, mobile-friendly & should have call to action.

- **Validity:** All pages should be embedded with social media buttons & pages should be W3c Valid.

- **Coding Hierarchy:** Take care of coding hierarchy & mention comments for each page while coding.

- **Loading Speed:** Check the loading time of the website with the Pingdom Website Speed Test or PageSpeed Insights. If bad, rectify the issues as soon as possible.

- **Broken Links:** Rectify broken links on the website and the URL link should be as per SEO parameters.

- **JavaScript:** Minify all JavaScript.

- **301, 302, 404 & Canonical Tags:** Start using 301 redirects to transfer old webpages or removed pages to new pages. There should be 404 error pages for non-existing content searches. Besides this, take care of Canonical Tags wherever required.

- **Hosting Account:** Choose a good hosting account; the server should be responsive. Example: GoDaddy.com and SiteGround.com.

- **Robot.txt & Sitemap.xml:** Check Robot.txt & Sitemap.xml existence.

- **Text/HTML Ratio:** Check out keyword density, keyword proximity and Text/HTML ratio. Improve them, if required.

- **Schema Markup:** Implement Schema Markup for search engines to crawl your content in an organized manner and display it correctly.

- **No Follow & No Index:** Use no follow and no index directives carefully on your website.

- **Trust Flow and Citation Flow:** Check the Trust Flow and Citation Flow of the website and improve them as per requirement.

- **Major Off-Page Criteria:** Check Domain Authority, Page Authority, Social Sharing, Link Juice, and Anchor text.

- **Uniformity of Keywords:** Good keyword analysis brings great SEO results. It is not the only consideration, but a major player in SEO as complete web pages are full of content, images, tags, and titles. With qualitative content, the right use of keywords throughout the pages will slowly and steadily improve the web page rank.

"You can use the Google Keyword Planner, Alexa's Competitor Keyword Matrix tool, Google Suggest, or Keywordtool.io. Google Ads Keyword Planner is free as you sign up for Google Ads.

Signing up for 7 days advance trial plan of the Alexa site gives the full insight into competitors' keywords. Other tools for keyword research are KwFinder, LongTailPro, SEMrush, and Moz Keyword Research Tool."

- **Blog, a Must in SEO**

Blogging is the best way to drive genuine traffic to your website as a blog is mandatory when it comes to search engine optimization. You should do in-depth research on topics concerning your web page content.

Try to read a lot of competitors' sites to know what blog exactly works and how to blog in the best manner to drive traffic. Build an authentic image among subscribers and visitors.

Even you can become a podcast guest or start guest posting to build a genuine brand among the audience.

- **Earn Good Backlink/Inbound Links**

You need to work hard to get good backlinks (Inbound Links). Try to get backlinks from high domain authority websites from a relevant field which increases the quality votes for your website.

- **Local SEO for Your Brand**

As a beginner, you should register your brand with Google My Business, Bing, and other local search engines to get better visibility. Add your business name & address on the main pages of your website like the home page and contact us page.

- **Outbound links & Internal Links**

Create only relevant outbound links that relate to your content. Create proper internal links throughout the website for user-friendliness that provides easy navigation for both users and search engines.

- **GDPR compliance**

GDPR compliance is playing an essential role in safeguarding visitor's credentials. It will also influence the website ranking.

- **Submissions**

Apart from on-page optimization, to improve domain authority, you need to opt for Website Link Submissions, Article Submissions, Social

Bookmarking, Video Submissions, Profile Submissions, Forum Posting, Blog Commenting, and Wiki Submissions.

- **Analytics**

Set up the Google Search Console, install Bing Webmaster Tools, Google Analytics, and install Yoast SEO (WordPress Users Only)

- **Avoid Black Hat Strategies**

If you are interested in going a long way and want great results, follow white hat strategies instead of black hat strategies.

- **Chrome Extensions & Tools**

The list of tools and extensions are:

- **Chrome Extensions**

  MozBar, BuzzSumo, Page Analytics, SEOquake, Ninja Outreach Lite, LinkMiner, Alexa Traffic Rank, etc.

- **SEO Tools**

  Google Search Console, Google Analytics, Ubersuggest, Semrush, Kissmetrics, Ahrefs, Alexa Competitor Keyword Matrix, Google Ads Keyword Planner, SEO Book Keyword Density Analyzer, KwFinder, LongTailPro,

SEMrush, Moz Keyword Research Tool & Pingdom Website Speed Test, PageSpeed Insights, Grammarly, and Copyscape Plagiarism Checker.

Social Media Marketing & Optimization

Social Media Marketing

Social Media Marketing is the process of creating high-quality content. It is customized in the context of the individual channel to attract more engagements or conversions on different social media platforms.

Example: Facebook, LinkedIn, Twitter, Instagram, Reddit, YouTube, Snapchat, Tumblr, Quora & Pinterest.

These are the means to gain website traffic and are the important channels for customer acquisition, customer retention, and re-marketing.

Thus, we can say that social media marketing helps to increase brand exposure and broaden customer reach.

Social Media Optimization

The social media world is expanding faster than any other online space, and it is not easy to maintain the pace. **Social Media Optimization** is an essential component of SMM with a strategy to gain unique visitors to any website.

It could be RSS feed, social media sharing button, activities like the status update, tweets, blog posts, etc.

After SMO, you proceed for SMM to publicize and share high-quality content on various social media platforms for your audience.

Social Media Optimization is the process of optimization of a website for various social media channels. It integrates social sharing tools to a website, directing website links to social media channels or vice versa.

SMO makes the website more social media-friendly. Visitors find it easy to share web links through social media channels. The process includes on-page optimization, i.e., refining the interface and usability of a website.

"In short, SMO is a process of optimization of the website and social media profiles to attract more organic engagements, whereas Social Media Marketing is the further step to SMO."

SMM includes all activities that are done offsite (other platforms). Facebook, LinkedIn, Twitter, Instagram, Reddit, YouTube, Snapchat, Tumblr, Quora & Pinterest are not only the means to gain more traffic or conversion but also beneficial channels for customer acquisition, customer retention, and re-marketing.

Thus, Social Media Marketing promotes your website through different social media platforms. It includes both ways of paid and organic marketing.

"The list of social media networking sites includes Facebook, LinkedIn, Twitter, Instagram, Reddit, YouTube, Snapchat, Tumblr, Quora, Pinterest, WhatsApp, Facebook Messenger, WeChat, QQ, QZone, Skype, Viber, Snapchat, Line, Baidu Teiba, and Sina Weibo."

Tools for Social Media Marketing

Every digital marketer has a core interest in social media marketing tools. I have listed out a few that are in no particular order.

"The marketing tools are Social Mention, Hootsuite, Followerwonk, TweetDeck, SumAll, Klout, TweetReach, Crowdfire, SocialPilot, Buffer, BuzzSumo, Cyfe, and SharedCount."

Content

Marketing

Content Marketing can be defined as concrete and strategic marketing approach that focuses on the creation and distribution of valuable, relevant & quality content. It attracts a specific audience – that drives profitable customer action.

In content marketing, you focus on the resolution of the issues of your audience by providing relevant quality content. But **Inbound Marketing** is a strategic utilization of tactics & strategies to attract potential customers to find your brand.

So, the necessary things for Inbound Marketing Strategy are Great Content, Website Optimization, Social Media Sharing, Blogs, Events, SEO Strategy, Email Marketing, Social Media Strategy, SEO Related Content, and so on.

In short, content marketing is a subset of inbound marketing, while inbound marketing is the superset of content marketing. Thus, this means it is inclusive of all content assets but is not limited to them.

In general, content marketing is an element of inbound marketing, so you cannot plan for inbound marketing without content marketing.

Content Marketing Strategies

Undoubtedly, the following steps will surely help you to make your inbound and content marketing strategies.

Set Target: One Goal at a Time

You should set a target for your content marketing plan. Whether it is **content marketing strategy or inbound marketing strategy,** you should be clear about your outcome result.

"It could be to grow subscribers, branding, customer acquisition & sales, lead conversion, or customer retention."

Quality Content: Win-Win Strategy

When we talk about quality content, it is the freshness and uniqueness. There is no substitute for quality content that drives massive traffic to your website.

You can opt for infographics, white papers, eBooks, blog posts, social media posts, videos, podcasts, live streaming, & webinars.

You need to craft topics that serve the purpose for both readers and company/brand.

Focus: Audience

The ultimate goal of marketing strategies is to acquire and retain customers. You must have a clear idea of the niche that you are going to serve.

Following the responsive market, do more research on high domain authority websites of your niche to know what type of content is getting more response.

These sorted out queries will clarify your doubts about your ideal & potential readers.

"For inbound marketing, research on a complete list of keywords, use tools like **Google Keyword Planner, Google Trends, KwFinder, LongTailPro, SEMrush, and Moz Keyword Research Tool.** Even you can research hashtags of trending topics on social media of your niche."

For freshness and uniqueness of the content, always use **grammar** and **plagiarism checker tools.** It will avoid duplicate content.

Advertise: Promote Your Brand

In today's scenario, you cannot avoid paid advertising. You have to select the platforms where your audience has more presence.

Opt for Google Ads, Facebook, Social Media Marketing, and YouTube Advertisement for branding, customer acquisition, and retention.

Maintain a balance between your advertising & budget to reach your ideal audience. For videos, you have many options to create a broad audience base; like **YOUTUBE & VIMEO.**

You should submit blog posts on high domain authority websites like Quora and keep answering the queries to build a brand image.

Monitor Performance: Mark Your Steps

Tracking performance is a mandatory part of any marketing strategy. With these metrics, you can get complete information about unique visitors, first-time visitors, social media response, and readers' engagement.

*"Use Basic Tools like **Google Analytics, Google Search Console, Facebook Analytics, and Hootsuite** to monitor your results."*

Blogging

Start from Scratch & Make Money

Blogging is one of the activities that has been made prevalent today due to the proliferation of the internet. The good thing about blogging is the fact that some people do it as a hobby, while others make it a means of livelihood.

The number of bloggers is expected to reach **31.7 million in 2020 (Statista)**. Blogging is quite lucrative and you must know how to make money off it.

Many people go into blogging without proper knowledge, so they are not sure of results. If you are thinking of setting up a blog and you have decided to do a little more research before starting, then you have set yourself up for success.

You must know how to set a blog properly before embarking on the task.

Start a Blog

Pick the Best Blog Category

Decide the blog category that suits your knowledge and passion. Delivery of the best content is of high importance.

Choose a Good Domain Name

You need to choose a domain name that is suitable for your blog. You can check on Go Daddy and accordingly choose .com, .in, and so on.

Choose a Hosting Account

Hosting account is a significant factor, so choose wisely. You can opt for shared hosting in the beginning. Go Daddy, Site Ground, and Blue Host are the few options.

WordPress Theme

There are many free and paid WordPress themes but prefer to choose a paid theme that is pocket-friendly. Sometimes there are many plugin issues with a free theme, so one-time theme selection is a better option.

Look for theme options available on websites like ThemeForest, Colorlib, etc.

Crux of Great Blogging

High-quality content with proper keywords will enhance Google ranking. You have to look into the following parameters.

Title – Prefer a good title with one focused keyword to write a neat blog post

Meta Description – Nicely crafted meta description helps search engines to rank your blog post higher

Start and End – The beginning of the article should be in a relevant context with the correct use of keywords and end the post with a conclusion

Tags – Take care of H1, H2, H3 tags throughout the blog post

Keywords – Use proper keywords throughout the post without stuffing

Featured Image – Use an attractive featured image for your post. Get free photos from Canva, Pixabay, etc.

Plugins – Few plugins are very much essential for

your WordPress website like All in one SEO, SEO Yoast, Google AdSense, Email Marketing Plugin, Total Cache, and so on.

Driving Website Traffic

Driving traffic is not an easy job.

You need to be more focused on driving traffic via email marketing, search engine optimization, social media marketing, submissions, and so on. Submissions include a list of work like link submissions, blog submissions, blog commenting, forum posting, etc.

Email Marketing

Email marketing is an excellent marketing strategy, especially for small businesses. They improve the efficiency of your marketing, leading to more leads and higher conversion rates.

Start your email marketing campaign and grab the attention of your visitors. A few examples of them are **MailChimp, ConvertKit, Constant Contact, and GetResponse.**

Social Media Marketing

Social media marketing creates a huge audience base, generates leads, and converts into sales.

Each social media platform can direct traffic to your website and make your blogging site a huge success.

Search Engine Optimization

It will surely help you in the long run. On-page optimization and off-page optimization techniques can bring your website to rank 1 in Google search results.

SEO is not a one-day work but slowly and steadily, you can make it happen.

Make Money from Blogging

Everyone wants to make money. How to make money online with zero loss strategy? The answer is **Google AdSense.** Once your website is ready and has 15-20 good quality blog posts, you can opt for **Google AdSense.**

With the growth of your website visitors and credibility, you can start **Affiliate Marketing** that generates enormous revenue.

Visit your niche sellers and most of them are nowadays open to affiliate marketers.

Why your niche or related sellers?

If you want to start affiliate marketing and you write blogs for a specific niche, then the chances of conversion are more with the same niche within a short period. It will enhance your experience.

After a particular stage, bloggers start selling their products and services, so those options are also open for you.

Affiliate

Marketing

Earn with Affiliate Marketing

When it comes to online earning, the most discussed term is **"Affiliate Marketing"** and many bloggers rely on affiliate marketing to make huge passive income.

What does this exactly mean and how does it work?

Affiliate Marketing includes the process of promoting other company's products. In return, you will receive a piece of profit in the form of commission for each sale that you make by promoting it.

If you choose the right way, you can generate a considerable income with affiliate marketing.

Connections

Before starting with affiliate marketing, you should know the primary relationships involved in affiliate marketing. The three key relations used are **merchant, affiliate, and customer.**

The complete affiliate marketing moves around the merchant, affiliate, and customer. If a customer clicks on the link on an affiliate website for sale, then the affiliate receives a commission from the merchant.

Terms

Affiliate Link, Affiliate Network, Affiliate Manager, Cloaking, CPM, CPC, CPA, Impression, Landing page, PPL, PPC, SEO, ROI, Split Testing, and so on.

Plugins

A few WordPress plugins that will support your affiliate marketing program are Broken Link Checker, Thirsty Affiliates, etc.

Affiliate Marketing Networks

Amazon Affiliate Program

Amazon affiliate program is the most discussed affiliate program among bloggers and marketers.

Of course, it is profitable and you can choose it. You can promote Amazon products on your website, social media, etc.

Email marketing can be a great option if you want to reach the audience within a limited budget.

The commission varies from one category to another. It provides all the tools and resources like affiliate links, banners, and reports for facilitating the promotion.

You can surely start with the Amazon affiliate program as it will be profitable if you choose the right products and promote them in the right way.

Click Bank

Click Bank is one of the best marketplaces for affiliate marketers.

There are many products on click bank and you can create an affiliate link of your choice.

Choose the products intelligently as it becomes challenging to make a choice.

C J Affiliate and Shareasale

C J Affiliate has thousands of products to promote and you can promote any product of your choice. Sign up and get product links and banners for promotion.

Shareasale provides all tools for promotion and here you can get complete statistics and reports.

*"The other examples of affiliate marketing networks are **Jvzoo**, **PeerFly**, **Maxbounty**, and **Rakuten**."*

Promotion Methods

The various promotion methods that you can try for affiliate marketing are listed below:

PPC (Pay per Click) and Banner Ads

Display ads for particular keywords can be one of the options to generate sales, but many affiliate programs don't allow PPC due to their policies. However, a few affiliate programs allow PPC campaigns on Bing.

Anyways you have an option to earn a lot of money with your dedicated efforts.

Banner ads can also be an option where you need to choose a product and find a high traffic website where you can display ads.

Example: BuySellAds and AdClerks

SEO

Many affiliate sites manage their sales with the help of SEO.

In SEO driven affiliate marketing, the main focus is to get traffic from different search engines.

Content-Based Affiliate Marketing

It is about writing content for your affiliate product and the best way is blogging. It drives traffic to your blog and generates affiliate sales in return. Email marketing could be an option to get in touch with your audience, so keep on building your email lists.

Conclusion

After going a long way from SEO to Affiliate Marketing, you might have queries about your business. One strategy may work for one business, while others may not.

So, when you are trying to set up your business, you should know these fundamentals to build a brand.

Try to develop a road map and ROI oriented marketing strategy as there can be a limitation of budget. Identify your business as B2B or B2C and accordingly make a plan for a long and short run. Better ideation and execution will help to build your brand locally and globally.

Benefits:

- Increases the pool of customers
- Improves brand awareness
- Increases customer reach
- Gives an edge over your competitors

Career-oriented professionals have to work on these areas to make money and develop a personal brand as a marketer.

In this digital age, whether it is about the organizations or the professionals, all need to equip themselves with digital marketing skills.

There are numerous free online digital marketing courses and certifications.

"The best digital marketing courses are Google Digital Unlocked, WordStream (PPC University), Alison, and SkillShop (formerly Google Academy for Ads). You can keep on updating your skills and start generating passive income."

I wish and hope that all strategies work perfectly for you.

"Never Stop Due to Hurdles, Keep on Exploring Opportunities"

Author's Note

In closing, I would love to know whether this book was helpful to you or not. If you find it interesting and a good piece of content, kindly share your honest review of this book.

Share your thoughts to me and it will be my pleasure to reply to you personally.

I hope Digital Marketing Beats has provided some value to your career and business. Have a great journey of success!

Website: www.digitaltarannum.com
Email: info@digitaltarannum.com
Academy: https://www.digitaltarannum.com/digital-tarannum-academy/
Courses: https://www.digitaltarannum.com/courses/

Thank you!
Tarannum Khan